Zoom In on Farm Animals

Cows

Leo Statts

abdopublishing.com

Published by Abdo Zoom™, PO Box 398166, Minneapolis, Minnesota 55439.

Printed in the United States of America, North Mankato, Minnesota
092016
012017

THIS BOOK CONTAINS
RECYCLED MATERIALS

Cover Photo: Shutterstock Images
Interior Photos: iStockphoto, 1, 5, 13, 15, 17, 19; Shutterstock Images, 6, 10, 12–13; Global Pics/iStockphoto, 7; Ruud Morijn/iStockphoto, 8; Frank van den Bergh/iStockphoto, 9; Artem Zakharov/Shutterstock Images, 11; Oleg Krugliak/Shutterstock Images, 14; Ralf Gosch/Shutterstock Images, 18; Red Line Editorial, 20 (left), 20 (right), 21 (left), 21 (right)

Editor: Emily Temple
Series Designer: Madeline Berger
Art Direction: Dorothy Toth

Publisher's Cataloging-in-Publication Data
Names: Statts, Leo, author.
Title: Cows / by Leo Statts.
Description: Minneapolis, MN : Abdo Zoom, 2017. | Series: Farm animals |
Includes bibliographical references and index.
Identifiers: LCCN 2016948665 | ISBN 9781680799040 (lib. bdg.) |
ISBN 9781624024900 (ebook) | ISBN 9781624025464 (Read-to-me ebook)
Subjects: LCSH: Cows--Juvenile literature.
Classification: DDC 636.2--dc23
LC record available at http://lccn.loc.gov/2016948665

Table of Contents

Cows

Cows are also called cattle.
Most live on farms.
More than 1 billion cows
live around the world.

Body

Cows come in different colors.

Most are black,
brown, or white.

Some cows have spots.

These are also called **markings**.

Food

Cows eat a lot.

They eat about 50 pounds (23 kg) of food each day.

Cows eat hay and grass.

They also eat **grain**.

Farm Life

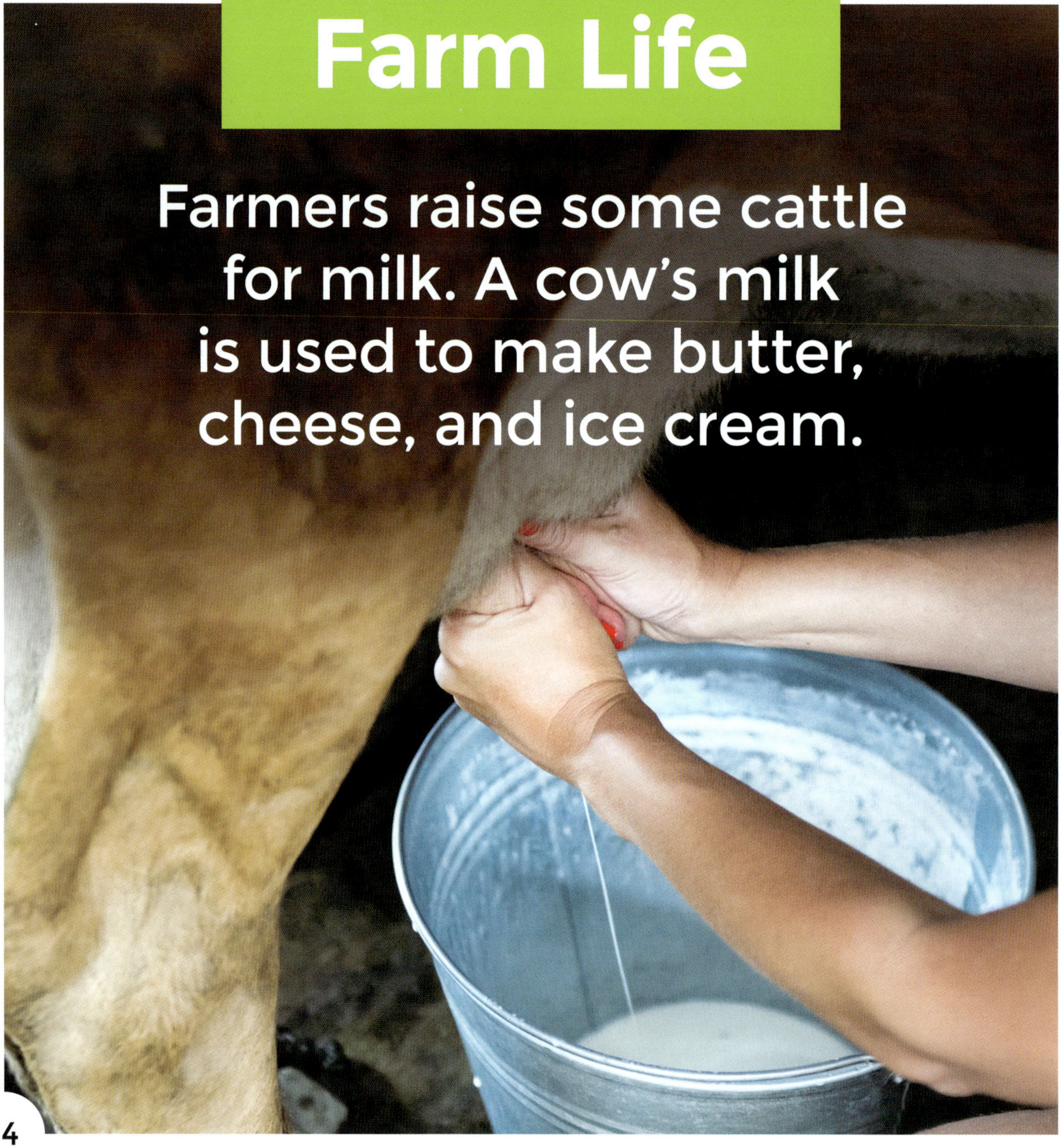

Farmers raise some cattle for milk. A cow's milk is used to make butter, cheese, and ice cream.

These are called **dairy** products.

Other cattle are raised for **beef** or leather. Sometimes cattle are used as work animals. They carry things or pull wagons.

Names

Male cattle are bulls or steers.

Females are called cows or heifers. Babies are **calves**.

Quick Stats

Average Weight

A bull weighs more than two soda vending machines.

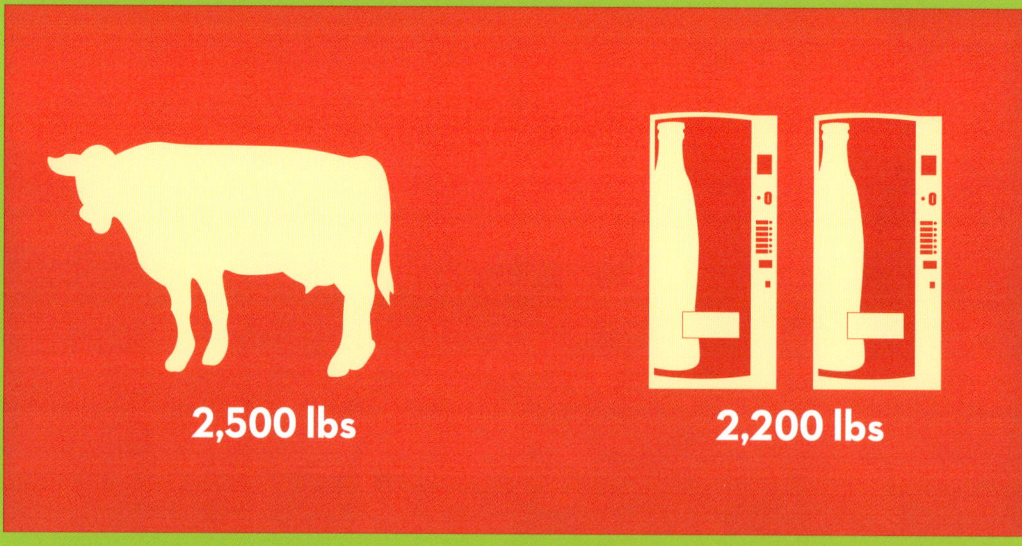

Quick Stats

Average Weight

A female cow weighs more than a soda vending machine.

Glossary

beef - meat that comes from cows.

calves - baby animals.

dairy - made from milk.

grain - the seeds of plants that are used for food.

marking - a mark or pattern of marks on an animal's fur, feathers, or skin.

Booklinks

For more information on cows, please visit booklinks.abdopublishing.com

Abdo Zoom

Zoom In on Animals!

Learn even more with the Abdo Zoom Animals database. Check out abdozoom.com for more information.

Index